the
hip handbag
book

25
Easy-to-make
Totes, Purses,
and Bags

the hip

25 Easy-to-make Totes, Purses, and Bags

handbag book

by SHERRI HAAB

with illustrations by
NINA EDWARDS

WATSON-GUPTILL PUBLICATIONS/NEW YORK

Senior Acquisitions Editor: Julie Mazur
Project Editor: Anne McNamara
Designer: Georgia Rucker
Production Manager: Hector Campbell

Photography by Dan Haab

First published in 2004 by
Watson-Guptill Publications, Inc.
a division of VNU Business Media, Inc.
770 Broadway, New York, NY 10003
www.wgpub.com

Flower Power purse project (pages 40–41) first appeared in the March/April 2001 issue of American Girl magazine.

Library of Congress Control Number: 2004106250

Printed in China

First printing, 2004

3 4 5 6 7 8 / 11 10 09 08 07 06 05

acknowledgments

To my husband Dan, thank you for the beautiful photographs

Thank you to Rachel and Michelle for your creative ideas
and photography assistance, and to David for your patience

Many thanks to the editorial and design staff at
Watson-Guptill for their dedication to this project

And thanks to all of the manufacturers who supplied
products and technical advice for the projects in this book

table of contents

8 introduction
   it's in the bag

10 tools and techniques
   all you need to know

20 taking it easy
   cute styles anyone can do

22 **LETTER PERFECT** monogram jean pocket purse

24 **SIGN OF THE TIMES** scorpio jean pocket purse

26 **FINDERS KEEPERS** secondhand bag with appliqués

28 **ON THE LINE** corduroy feather bag

30 **PRETTY IN PINK** cosmetic bag purse

32 **SCARLET FEVER** red flower bag

34 **THE HEAT IS ON** canvas bag with iron-on

36 **SOFT TOUCH** fleece bags

38 gearing up
so cool, sew simple

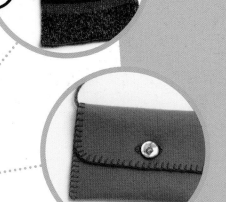

40 **FLOWER POWER** ribbon purses

42 **SWEET THINGS** cookie bag purse

44 **ANIMAL INSTINCT** faux fur bag

46 **FAUX EASY** funky fur purse

48 **PUT A SOCK IN IT** sock coin purse

51 **A SHORE THING** placemat beach bag

54 **BAG-ALONG** felt purse

56 **COLOR BLOCKS** geometric felt purse

58 **CELL MATE** embroidered cell phone bag

62 **OUTSIDE THE BOX** stationery box bag

64 bring it on
nothing can stop you now

66 **VINTAGE VISIONS** collage tote

70 **SEEING THINGS** clear laminated flower purse

74 **NEWS FLASH** laminated newspaper bag

78 **STICK TO IT** duct tape bag

82 **QUICK SILVER** trapezoid duct tape bag

86 **STRIPE IT RICH** striped duct tape purse

90 **PLASTIC FANTASTIC** grocery bag purse

94 shop talk
where to go for what

introduction

it's in the bag

If you are like most of us, you carry your entire life inside your purse. Handbags and purses are more than simple sacks to carry our stuff around in. They're how we say who we are, what we like, and what we *feel* like today. The truth is, handbags are your best-friend accessory—you don't want to go anywhere without them!

The great thing about making your own handbags is that each bag is uniquely your own. You can make handbags to specially match your favorite outfits, or you can design an entire look around an out-of-this-world bag. Best of all, making the bag itself is a lot of fun.

The projects in this book are broken down into three sections. The first section, *taking it easy*, has an assortment of great bags that are quick and easy to make. Got a little more time on your hands? Then you're ready for the next batch of projects, *gearing up*. You'll find how with just a few basic stitches you can make anything from a cell phone purse to a canvas tote. Okay, so now you feel like a challenge? The last section, *bring it on*, has a selection of amazing purses that you'll be proud to say you made yourself.

Create a bag for anywhere and anything—whether a trip to the beach or a night out with friends. Recycle old materials to make bags out of plastic, fabric, or snack food containers. Personalize your bags with painted designs, magazine pictures, gems, and beads. The idea is to have as much fun creating the bag as using it. So, let's get started!

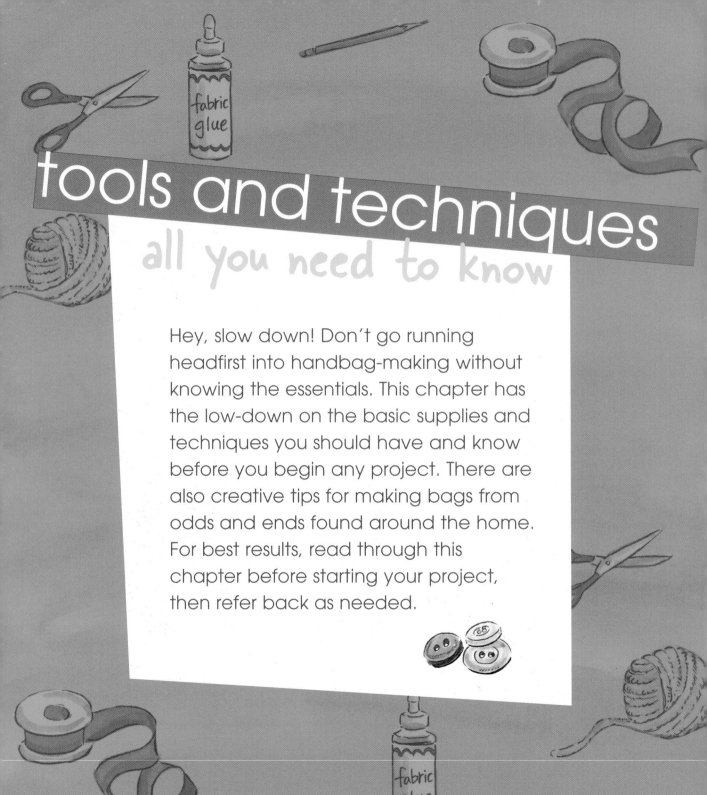

tools and techniques

all you need to know

Hey, slow down! Don't go running headfirst into handbag-making without knowing the essentials. This chapter has the low-down on the basic supplies and techniques you should have and know before you begin any project. There are also creative tips for making bags from odds and ends found around the home. For best results, read through this chapter before starting your project, then refer back as needed.

tools and supplies

Any project is easier with the right tools on hand. This section explains what tools and supplies you should have in your craft kit. Make sure you have all of your materials ready before you start working on a project. Nothing is worse than being in the middle of something and having to stop and run to the store! Check out the section, Shop Talk, on page 94 for specific product tips and shopping advice.

CUTTERS

- **Scissors** You should have a good pair of paper scissors for cutting paper, cardboard, and laminate, as well as sewing scissors for cutting fabric, felt, cord, and ribbon. Never use fabric scissors on paper; it will dull the blades. (It's a good idea to label the handles with tape or tie-on tags so you'll remember which pair is which.)

- **Wire cutters or old nail clippers** Wire cutters have short, straight blades that snip wires with ease. They can be found in the jewelry making section in craft stores. While not as sharp as wire cutters, an old pair of nail clippers will also do the trick.

- **Hole punch** These are sold in office supply and craft stores in ⅛ and ¼ inch sizes. In addition to circles, there are specialty punches in diamond, heart, and square shapes.

- **Needle tool or large needlepoint or tapestry needle** Available in fabric and craft stores, these tools are useful for poking holes for paper fasteners or wire to pass through.

hot tip

Organize your supplies in plastic containers, boxes, or drawers so setting up your work area will be super quick and easy.

GLUES AND ADHESIVES

- **Fabric glue** Fabric glue is specially designed to glue fabric and fabric-like materials together, including ribbon, rickrack, and felt.

- **Gem or jewel glue** Use gem or jewel glue to attach beads, gems, buttons, and plastic decorations.

- **White craft glue** This all-purpose glue dries clear and is great to use on paper, cardboard, and other materials. You can even use it to attach small items like sequins.

- **Liquid seam sealant** These specialty glues (Fray Check and Fray Stop are the two most common brands) hold loose threads in place and prevent fraying along cut edges of fabric and cord. Craft glue can also be used to seal cut fabric edges.

- **Decoupage glue** This glue is applied over the surface of some of the finished purses to add an extra layer of protection. Pour some into a small dish and use a paintbrush to coat the surface.

- **Double-stick tape** Double-stick tape is sticky on both sides, allowing you to attach paper or laminate neatly and easily.

purse handles and straps

You don't have to go to some special shop to find materials for purse handles or straps. The following items are as easy to find as they are to work with:

- ✔ **Cord or ribbon** Sold in craft and fabric stores.
- ✔ **Shoelaces** Use old ones or buy new laces at variety stores.
- ✔ **Chain** Available at home supply or hardware stores.
- ✔ **Plastic-coated craft wire** Packages of colorful craft wire can be purchased in craft and hobby stores.
- ✔ **Plastic and wooden beads** (to use on wire handles) These can be bought individually or by the bag in craft and fabric stores.

starting from the ground up
purse-making materials and where to find them

- **Cosmetic bags**—Stores often give these bags away with make-up. Ask your mother or sister if they have any extras. Cosmetic bags are also sold in most department and drug stores.

- **Blue jeans**—Think twice before you toss out those never-fit-me-again blue jeans. Roomy denim pockets make great handbags.

- **Boxes**—Boxes come in almost every size and shape imaginable, and many are ideal for making into handbags. Look around your home, in craft and stationery stores, and at flea markets for cool boxes, tins, or other containers.

- **Plastic bags**—Use your imagination! Yes, that's a grocery bag, but it is so much more! Stop and think before you throw away those used plastic bags—you might be holding your next great purse.

- **Tape**—Duct tape and clear packing tape, sold at almost any variety store, can be used to make sleek-looking handbags.

- **Fabric and trims**—Check out craft and fabric stores for good buys on fabrics, such as felt, canvas, and corduroy—and trims, such as ribbon and rickrack.

- **Office supplies and stationery**—Find office essentials, such as laminate sheets, contact paper, and decorative papers at stationery, paper goods, and office supply stores.

- **Secondhand bags**—Creative touches can turn gently used purses into hip fashion accessories. Used handbags are easy to find in thrift stores and yard sales. Or you can offer to help mom clean out her closet!

- **Housewares**—Take nothing for granted! Inexpensive plastic placemats, easy to find in variety and kitchen stores, are all you need to make sturdy, water-resistant totes.

MISCELLANEOUS TOOLS

- **Ruler** You'll need a ruler to measure materials, make patterns, draw straight lines, and lots more.

- **Pencil** Pencils are an absolute must for writing and marking. Keep a jar of sharpened pencils handy so you'll always have one when you need it.

- **Paintbrushes** Paintbrushes come in assorted sizes. Use medium-sized brushes to apply glue over large areas. Small round brushes are great for painting detailed designs.

- **Magnets** Round disk magnets, like the ones used for refrigerator magnets, are a neat way to close your purse. Use gem glue to attach the magnets, letting the glue dry completely to keep the magnet in place.

- **Velcro** Velcro can be sewn or glued on handbags to secure flaps.

- **Rhinestones** Flat-back rhinestones will dress up any design. Use gem or jewel glue to attach the stones to your bag.

- **Buttons and beads** Buttons and beads can be sewn or glued on handbags. Find ones that match the style of the bag you are making. You can also use buttons to close your purse and beads to make a purse handle.

- **Beaded trims, ribbon, and rickrack** Fabric stores carry all kinds of trim, from jumbo rickrack to dainty lace ribbon. Fabric glue is good for attaching most trims, but you might need gem glue for beaded trims. Press trims in place as you glue, then let them sit flat until the glue has set.

- **Fabric paints** Fabric paints are very popular and are available at most craft and fabric stores. Dimensional, iridescent, pearl, neon, glow-in-the-dark, and glitter paints offer lots of choices. Most fabric paints become permanent when heated, meaning they won't wash out. Always follow the manufacturer's instructions when using paint on your purse or handbag.

- **Paper fasteners** Use paper fasteners, available in office supply, stationery, and variety stores, to attach handles and straps to bags (see Working with Paper Fasteners, page 18).

basic techniques

The handbags in this book are easy enough for even first-time crafters and sewers to make. Here are some basic techniques to get you started.

GLUING

When working with glue, be sure to cover your work surface with plastic, newspaper, or even an old magazine. Pour some glue into a plastic dish, then use a toothpick to apply it to your bag. This will help you from accidentally squeezing out a big blob of glue and ruining a project. Be sure to use the right glue for the material, whether fabric, gem, or white craft glue. When working with glue, always be patient and let the glue dry completely.

SEWING

The first step in successful sewing is choosing the right thread. **All-purpose sewing thread** is good for most hand sewing and for attaching the cord. Use **heavy-duty thread** on very thick fabrics, like canvas and corduroy. Or make sewing thread sturdier by doubling the thread. (To double your thread, cut a long piece and push one end through the eye of a needle. Knot the two ends together to form a big loop.) To hide your stitchwork, choose a thread color that matches your fabric. **Embroidery floss** is good for both embroidery and for making bigger stitches. It is made up of six little threads that you can pull apart—you then use only two or three strands. **Craft Thread** by DMC is similar to embroidery floss, but does not separate. It is easy to work with and comes in a variety of colors, including metallic colors. Embroidery floss and Craft Thread are good to use on felt. The colorful stitches can be used as part of the bag design or simply to decorate the felt.

hot tip

Cord or ribbon may fray on the cut ends. Coat the ends with white glue or a liquid seam sealant like Fray Check (page 13). Let the glue dry before attaching the cord to the purse.

THREADING THE NEEDLE Before starting any sewing stitch, cut a long piece of thread or floss. Carefully put one end through the hole (called the "eye") of the needle. Pull it through until there is one long and one short tail. Make a knot at the end of the long tail.

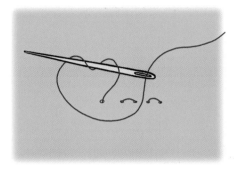

FINISHING KNOT When you are done sewing, wrap the thread around the needle twice and pull the thread tightly to finish.

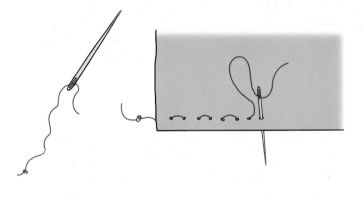

THE RUNNING STITCH This is the most basic of stitches used to sew two pieces of fabric together. Knot the thread and stitch up through the fabric and then back down through the fabric. Continue making stitches in and out of the fabric to make a line of evenly spaced stitches.

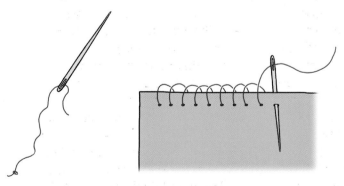

THE WHIPPED STITCH This stitch holds two finished fabric edges together. Insert the needle from the back of the fabric and pull through the front. Stitch over the top of the fabric edge(s) and back through to the front. Continue stitching over the edge of the fabric, making evenly spaced stitches.

WORKING WITH PAPER FASTENERS

Paper fasteners from an office supply store are great for securing cord, chain, wire, and other materials to purses. Push the pointed ends of the fastener through a piece of cord or chain, or twist wire around the fastener before attaching the fastener to the handbag.

◀ Poke the pointed ends of the fastener through a hole punched in the purse.

▶ Open the ends on the inside of the purse to secure.

WORKING WITH WIRE

Plastic-coated craft wire is available in different colors and gauges. The gauge tells you how thick or thin the wire is. A high gauge (18 to 28 gauge) means the wire is thin, and a low gauge (for example, 10 gauge) means it is thick. Use a low gauge, or thick wire, for making sturdy handles. Wire can also be used to close or decorate a handbag.

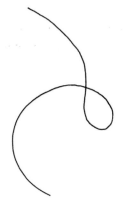

◀ To fasten a wire handle to your handbag, start about two inches from one end and bend the wire to form a loop, as shown.

▶ Twist the end around the wire several times to secure the loop. Clip off the excess wire with scissors or an old nail clipper.

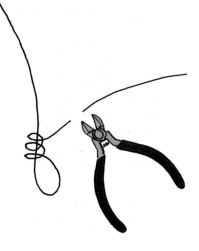

USING PATTERNS

The purses and bags in this book are made with simple shapes and measurements. Some projects include patterns that you should copy on a photocopier and enlarge as directed. Copy the pattern onto tracing paper, then use transfer paper to copy the lines onto the back side of the fabric or paper. Be sure to transfer all of the markings. You can also follow the directions to make the handbag pattern yourself. Simply use a ruler and pencil to measure and mark the cutting and folding lines as instructed.

hot tip

Making a paper pattern of your project before you begin is a good idea, whether the bag has a pattern provided or not. Measure and draw all of the lines, then fold the paper into the shape of the bag. This way you can check out the size and style of the bag before cutting the fabric, felt, or paper. Once you start the project, place the pattern over the fabric to use as a guide for folding and cutting. The best part about using a pattern is that you can use it over and over again. It will save you lots of time, and you won't need to make as many marks on the fabric or paper itself.

DRAWING STRAIGHT LINES

When making patterns, it is very important that your lines are drawn straight. If the lines aren't straight, the sides of the purse might not be even. This will not only make the bag look sloppy, but could also prevent it from closing correctly.

▶ Place the end of your ruler along the edge of the fabric or paper and make a mark at the measurement with a pencil. Slide the ruler to the left and repeat, marking the same measurement again a few inches away from the first. Now lay your ruler along the marks you made and draw a straight line connecting the marks.

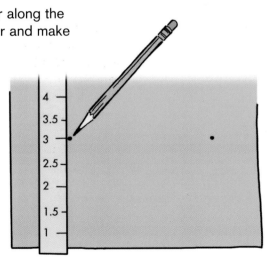

taking it easy

cute styles anyone can do

Do you shudder at the thought of sewing *anything*? Well, don't let that stop you! The handbags in this chapter require zero or only a tiny bit of sewing. You'll learn how to recycle items found around the home and in thrift stores to make great looking purses. Switch trims and decorations to make your bag a one-of-a-kind creation.

letter perfect

monogram jean pocket purse

This personalized bag is just the right size for carrying makeup, pencils and pens, or even a water bottle. Best of all, it's high fashion on the cheap. The purse is made by simply cutting the back pocket off of an old, throwaway pair of blue jeans.

what you need

- old, throwaway pair of jeans
- cord, about 36 inches
- white craft glue
- gem glue
- needle and thread
- pencil
- small paintbrush
- letter stencil or large letter cut from magazine or printed on a computer
- fabric paint in your choice of color
- small flat-back rhinestones
- fabric scissors
- sheet of wax paper or plastic wrap

▶▶ **STEP 1** Using fabric scissors, carefully cut the back pocket off of a used pair of blue jeans. Cut neatly around the pocket, being sure to cut evenly across the top.

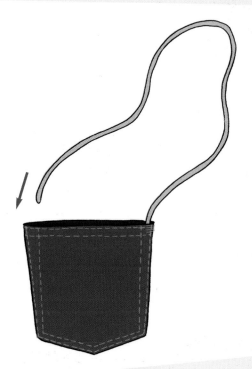

▶▶ STEP 2   Cut the cord to the length you want the purse strap to be (drape the cord over your shoulder to find the best length). Dip each end of the cord in white glue, then lay the cord on a sheet of wax paper or plastic wrap. Let the glue dry completely.

▶▶ STEP 3   With a needle and thread, sew the ends of the cord to the inside corners of the pocket, as shown.

hot tip
You can paint any design you like on the jean pocket purse. Look in craft stores for stencils in a wide variety of shapes and patterns.

▶▶ STEP 4   Place the cut-out letter or letter stencil on the front of the pocket. Use a pencil to trace the letter onto the fabric.

▶▶ STEP 5   Using a small paintbrush, carefully fill in the letter with paint. Let dry.

▶▶ STEP 6   Use gem glue to decorate the letter with small rhinestones. Let the glue dry completely.

sign of the times

scorpio jean pocket purse

It's in the stars: This bag is for you! You can find plastic decorations like this scorpion in variety and craft stores. Look for your astrological sign, or choose any fun shape you like.

what you need

- old, throwaway pair of jeans
- cord, about 36 inches
- white craft glue
- needle and thread
- fabric scissors
- plastic scorpion
- 5 buttons
- gem glue
- sheet of wax paper or plastic wrap

▶▶ **STEP 1** Using fabric scissors, carefully cut the back pocket off of a used pair of blue jeans. Cut neatly around the pocket, being sure to cut evenly across the top.

▶▶ **STEP 2** Cut the cord to the length you want the purse strap to be (drape the cord over your shoulder to find the best length). Dip each end of the cord in white glue, then lay the cord on a sheet of wax paper or plastic wrap. Let the glue dry completely.

▶▶ **STEP 3** With a needle and thread, sew the ends of the cord to the inside corners of the pocket, as shown.

▶▶ **STEP 4** Glue a plastic scorpion onto the front of the pocket with gem glue. Glue buttons along the top, as shown. Let dry overnight.

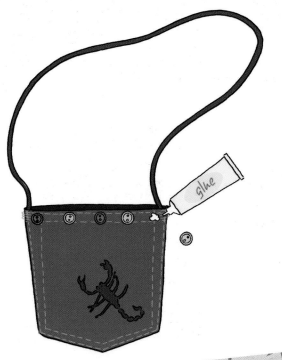

finders keepers

secondhand bag with appliqués

This is not your mother's handbag...well, maybe it *was*, but not anymore. This secondhand bag has a brand-new look thanks to pretty flower appliqués and a colorful Asian-style coin.

what you need

- black suede or fabric bag (a hand-me-down or secondhand store find)
- flower appliqués
- plastic Asian-style coin
- red plastic bead
- gold or silver string, about 6 inches
- gem glue
- fabric glue (optional)

hot tip

Plastic Asian-style coins can be purchased in variety and craft stores. Instead of a plastic coin, you can also use a large button.

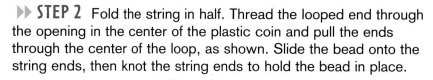

▶▶ **STEP 1** Arrange the appliqués on the front of the handbag. When you are satisfied with the design, use the fabric glue to secure them in place. Let the glue dry completely. If you are using iron-on appliqués, be sure to get an adult to help. Carefully follow the manufacturer's guidelines to iron the appliqués in place.

▶▶ **STEP 2** Fold the string in half. Thread the looped end through the opening in the center of the plastic coin and pull the ends through the center of the loop, as shown. Slide the bead onto the string ends, then knot the string ends to hold the bead in place.

▶▶ **STEP 3** Use gem glue to attach the beaded coin onto the bag flap. Let dry overnight.

on the line
corduroy feather bag

Corduroy has a casual look that's just right for school or hanging out with friends. All of your supplies, including feathers, wooden beads, and craft wire, are easy to find in craft stores. Small cosmetic bags are sold in department stores.

what you need

- small corduroy cosmetic bag with zipper
- 24-inch length of plastic-coated craft wire, 24 gauge
- wooden beads (1 large bag or enough to cover wire handle)
- feathers (as many as you want)
- large needle or needle tool
- old scissors or nail clippers
- fabric glue

▶▶ **STEP 1** Use a needle tool or large needle to carefully poke a hole in each side of the bag, as shown.

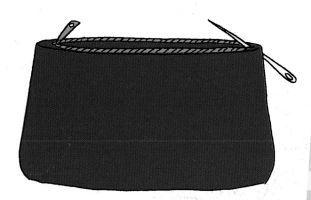

▶▶ STEP 2 Starting from the outside, poke one end of the wire through the first hole into the inside of the purse. Twist the wire end a few times around the length of wire to secure. Clip off any extra.

▶▶ STEP 3 String wooden beads onto the wire to make the handle. Stop when you have about 3 inches of wire left.

▶▶ STEP 4 Starting from the outside, poke the other end of the wire through the second hole. Twist the end around the length of wire to secure. Clip off any extra.

▶▶ STEP 5 Arrange the feathers on the front of the bag until you like the way they look. Glue them down one at a time.

▶▶ STEP 6 Carefully lay the purse flat and let dry overnight.

pretty in pink

cosmetic bag purse

This pink party purse couldn't be easier to make. Simply dress-up a plastic makeup bag with rickrack and faux pearls and you're ready to step out in style.

what you need

- small pink cosmetic bag with zipper
- 24-inch length of white plastic-coated craft wire, 24 gauge
- 8mm plastic pearls (1 large bag or enough to cover wire handle)
- rickrack, 18 inches
- large needle or needle tool
- old scissors or nail clippers
- gem glue

hot tip

Plastic cosmetic bags are easy to find in department and variety stores. Switch colors and trims to make bags to match your favorite outfits.

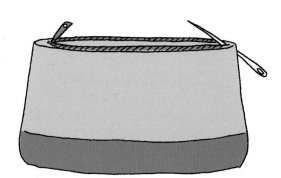

▶▶ **STEP 1** Use a large needle or needle tool to carefully poke a hole in each side of the bag, as shown.

▶▶ **STEP 2** Starting from the outside, poke one end of the wire through the first hole into the inside of the purse. Twist the wire end a few times around the length of wire to secure. Clip off any extra.

▶▶ **STEP 3** String plastic pearls onto the wire to make the handle. Stop when you have about 3 inches of wire left.

▶▶ **STEP 4** Starting from the outside, poke the other end of the wire through the second hole. Twist the end around the length of wire to secure. Clip off any extra.

▶▶ **STEP 5** Use gem glue to put rickrack across the front of the purse, as shown. Use the same glue to attach pearls along the top and bottom of the rickrack.

▶▶ **STEP 6** Carefully lay the purse on its back and let dry overnight.

what to stash in your bag for a party night

- ✔ lip gloss
- ✔ small mirror
- ✔ spending money
- ✔ cell phone
- ✔ comb or brush

scarlet fever
red flower bag

Everything is coming up roses on this flowery purse. Despite its fancy look, this bag is very easy to make. Save some fabric flowers to make matching hair accessories.

what you need

- small red cosmetic bag with zipper
- 24-inch length of white plastic-coated craft wire
- 8mm red round faceted beads (1 large bag or enough to cover wire handle)
- red fabric flowers (about 30–40)
- large needle or needle tool
- old scissors or nail clippers
- gem glue

▶▶ **STEP 1** Follow steps 1 through 4 for the Pretty in Pink purse on page 30. For step 3, string red beads onto the wire instead of plastic pearls.

▶▶ **STEP 2** Pull the red fabric flowers off of their stems, so you just have the flowers. Glue the flowers flat onto the bag. Continue until the whole bag is covered.

▶▶ **STEP 3** Carefully lay the purse flat and let dry overnight.

the heat is on

canvas bag with iron-on

This little canvas bag is just right for carrying school supplies like pens and pencils—even a calculator. Make bags with your favorite photos for yourself and to give as gifts to friends.

what you need

- small canvas tote bag (found at craft or fabric store)
- iron-on transfer paper (dark T-shirt transfer paper, available at craft and office supply stores)
- photos or pictures
- cord or shoelace, 24 or 30 inches
- white craft glue
- gem glue
- needle and thread
- scissors
- rickrack, beads, glitter, or jewels (optional)
- sheet of wax paper or plastic wrap

▶▶ **STEP 1** Follow the transfer paper manufacturer's instructions for printing a photo or picture onto T-shirt transfer paper.

▶▶ **STEP 2** If you want to make your own strap, carefully cut the handles from the tote.

▶▶ STEP 3 Before using an iron, always ask an adult for help. Follow the transfer paper manufacturer's instructions to iron the picture onto the front of the tote.

▶▶ STEP 4 Cut the cord to however long you want the strap to be (drape the cord over your shoulder to find the best length). Dip each end of the cord in white craft glue. Lay the cord on a sheet of wax paper or plastic wrap and let the glue dry completely.

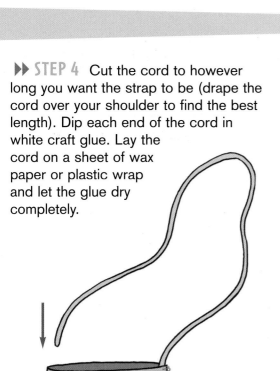

▶▶ STEP 5 Use a needle and thread to sew the ends of the cord to the inside corners of the bag.

▶▶ STEP 6 If you want, decorate the purse by gluing on rickrack, flat-backed jewels, or glitter.

soft touch *fleece bags*

These no-sew fleece bags are super light and fun to carry. The fleece is cut in strips and knotted along the sides to give the bag a frilly look. Look for fleece in lots of different patterns and colors in fabric stores.

what you need

- fleece fabric, ⅓ yard
- fabric scissors
- large sheet of paper
- ruler
- pencil

▶▶ **STEP 1** Make a paper pattern for the purse. With your ruler and pencil, measure and draw a 9 x 12 inch rectangle. If you want a larger purse, make the pattern 11 x 14 inches. Cut out your pattern.

▶▶ **STEP 2** Fold the fleece in half and lay your pattern on top. Cut around the pattern. You should end up with two same-size pieces of fleece.

▶▶ **STEP 3** Cut three long strips of fleece to braid for the strap. Cut the strips 1 inch wide by the length of the fleece.

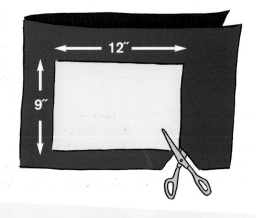

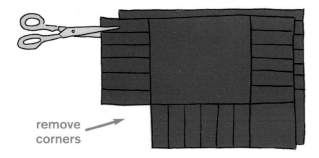

remove corners

STEP 4 Take the two purse pieces and lay them on top of each other. Use your scissors to snip a fringe around three sides, making sure you cut through both pieces of fleece. Each snip should be about 3 inches long. Leave 1 inch of fleece between each snip.

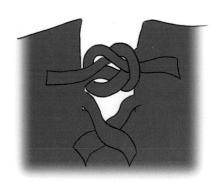

STEP 5 Start at one corner and tie each pair of strips together. Use a square knot, as shown. Continue knotting the strips together, working around the bag until all of the strips are tied.

STEP 6 Get the three long strips for the strap. Ask someone to hold them together tightly at one end (or take a safety pin and pin them to your backpack or the knee of your jeans). Braid the strips together until you are pleased with the length. Loop one end of the finished braid around the knotted strips at the top of one side of the bag and make a knot. Tie the other end of the braided strap to the other side of the bag.

gearing up
so cool, sew simple

Now that you've got the basics down, are you ready to put your skills to the test? The projects in this section use simple crafting techniques, like sewing and weaving. You'll also get creative with fun materials like felt, ribbon, and fur. And remember: You're the designer! Make your handbags in the colors and styles you like.

flower power

ribbon purses

Dainty flower appliqués add a garden-fresh look to these tiny ribbon purses. Use the same floral appliqués to spruce up everything from sneakers and jeans to book bags and t-shirts. If flowers aren't your thing, try other trims like buttons and bows.

what you need

- piece of wide ribbon, 6 inches long x 2 inches wide (for a bigger purse, use wider ribbon)
- fabric glue
- gem glue
- white craft glue
- cord or ribbon, about 36 inches
- needle and thread
- fabric scissors
- ribbon flowers, appliqués, buttons, or trim

▶▶ STEP 1 Lay the ribbon flat on a table, wrong side up (the "wrong" side is the back side of the ribbon). Fold each end down ⅜ inch and use the fabric glue to secure the folds. Let the glue dry.

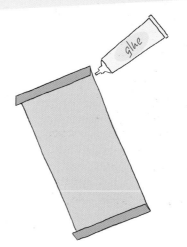

glue

STEP 2 Cut a piece of cord or ribbon for the strap (drape the ribbon or cord over your shoulder to find the best length). If using cord, tie a knot at each end to prevent fraying. Dip the ends in white glue and let dry.

STEP 3 Fold the purse ribbon in half with the glued edges at the top. Double thread your needle and knot the end (see page 16). Starting at one bottom corner, whipstitch up one side of the purse (see page 17).

STEP 4 As you reach the top, insert one end of the cord or ribbon strap and sew it to the inside of the purse. Knot the thread on the inside and snip off any extra. Repeat to sew up the other side of the purse and attach the other end of the strap.

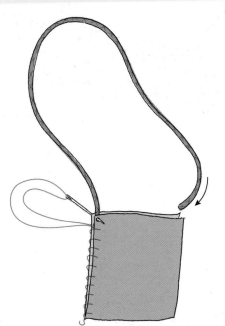

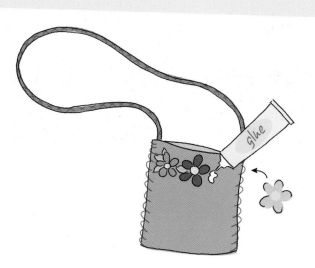

STEP 5 Use fabric glue to attach ribbon flowers or gem glue to attach buttons along the top edge of the purse. (Hint: slip a piece of plastic wrap inside the purse to keep the glue from soaking through the ribbon.)

STEP 6 Lay the purse flat and let dry overnight.

hot tip

With so many patterns and colors to choose from, there's a ribbon for every personality and style. For best results, choose either cotton ribbon (also called "craft ribbon") or grosgrain ribbon. These ribbons are extra strong and come in solid colors, prints, and stripes.

sweet things

cookie bag purse

Dare® Foods

Here's a project you'll want to sink your teeth into. These cookie bag purses are a tropical-breeze to make. Check out your local grocery store for colorful cookie bags and other soft-sided packages that you can transform into bright, bold purses.

what you need

- empty cookie bag
- clear Contact® brand self-adhesive covering paper (rolls 18 inches wide x 3 yards long are sold in craft stores)
- scissors
- round hole-punch
- cord or lace, about 24 inches
- ruler

▶▶ **STEP 1**

Before you start, make sure the cookie bag is clear of any crumbs. Carefully cut the top off of the bag to make a neat edge.

2″

fold along
dotted lines

2″

▶▶ **STEP 2** Now, cover the bag with Contact paper to make it extra sturdy. Measure the height of the bag and add 4 inches. Cut a piece of Contact paper to that measurement. Lay the paper sticky-side-up on your table. Lay the bag in the center of the paper, leaving 2 inches on top and bottom. Wrap the paper around the bag, pressing it in place with your hand inside the bag. Overlap the sides a bit and cut off the extra paper.

▶▶ **STEP 3** Trim the Contact paper along the top and bottom of the bag, leaving about 1 inch extra at the top and enough at the bottom to cover the bottom of the cookie bag. Cut a "V" shape out of the paper at each corner, on both the top and bottom.

▶▶ **STEP 4** Fold the Contact paper over the top edge of the bag and press in place inside the bag. Fold the paper over the bottom edge and press in place, covering the bottom of the bag.

▶▶ **STEP 5** Use the hole punch to punch two holes, one on each top side of the bag, as shown. Starting from the outside, poke one cord end through one hole and knot on the inside of the bag. Repeat to attach the other cord end on the other side of the bag.

hot tip

Instead of a cookie bag, you can also use a small gift bag or shopping bag.

cookie bag purse   43

animal instinct

faux fur bag

Zebra stripes for playful types. This fuzzy fur handbag will earn style points with everyone in your tribe. All it takes is a little cutting and gluing and you're ready to walk on the wild side.

what you need

- piece of faux fur, 9 x 12 inches
- fabric glue
- gem glue
- fabric scissors
- ruler
- pencil
- cord, about 24 inches
- needle and thread
- 2 strong disk magnets or Velcro® dots

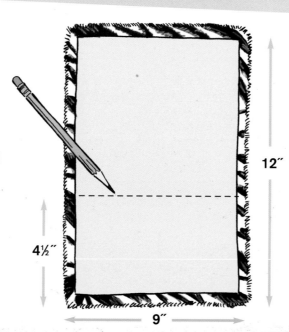

▶▶ STEP 1

Use the ruler and pencil to mark the wrong side of the faux fur with a rectangle measuring 9 x 12 inches (the "wrong side" is the side without fur). Cut out the rectangle with your fabric scissors.

12″

4½″

9″

▶▶ STEP 2

Lay the fur wrong-side-up with the short end nearest you. Measure up 4½ inches and draw a line across.

▶▶ **STEP 3** Fold the fabric up along that 4½-inch line. Apply a line of fabric glue along each side and press the fabric in place. Let dry overnight.

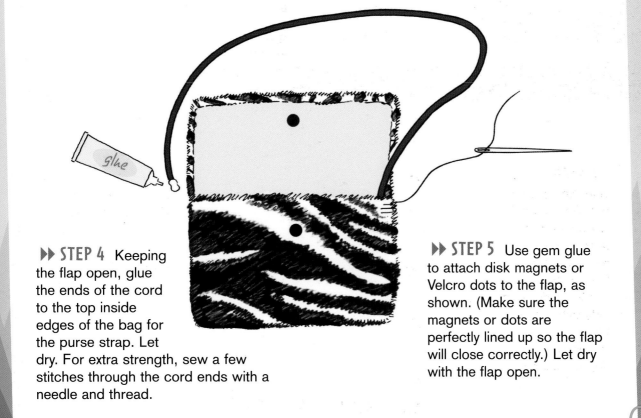

▶▶ **STEP 4** Keeping the flap open, glue the ends of the cord to the top inside edges of the bag for the purse strap. Let dry. For extra strength, sew a few stitches through the cord ends with a needle and thread.

▶▶ **STEP 5** Use gem glue to attach disk magnets or Velcro dots to the flap, as shown. (Make sure the magnets or dots are perfectly lined up so the flap will close correctly.) Let dry with the flap open.

faux easy

funky fur purse

It's a jungle out there! Get ready for school safari-style with a fabulous faux fur purse. You can find Funky Fur, a type of faux fur fabric, in a whole zoo-ful of animal prints, from leopard and zebra to lion and tiger. Each piece comes with a sheet of double-stick adhesive film, perfect for bag-making.

what you need

- sheet of Grafix brand Funky Fur
- sheet of Grafix brand Double-Stick 'N Stay (this sheet comes with the Funky Fur)
- 9 x 12-inch piece of felt
- fabric scissors
- ruler
- pencil
- cord, 24 inches
- gem glue
- needle and thread
- decorative button (optional)
- 2 strong disk magnets or Velcro® dots

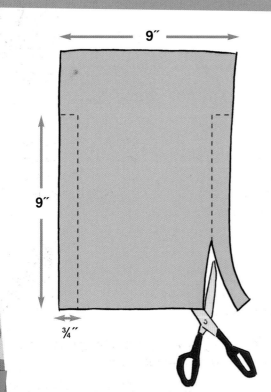

9″

9″

¾″

▶▶ **STEP 1** Use the ruler and pencil to mark a strip along each long side of the felt that's ¾ inches wide and 9 inches long, as shown. Cut the strip away on both sides.

▶▶ **STEP 2** Peel off one side of the protective paper from the double-stick adhesive and stick this to the wrong side of the Funky Fur (the "wrong side" is the side without fur).

▶▶ **STEP 3** Peel off the other side of the protective paper and stick the felt on top, making sure the edges of the felt and fur are perfectly lined up.

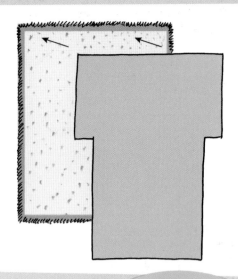

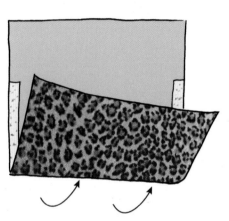

▶▶ **STEP 4** Fold up the bottom edge of the fur to form the purse, as shown. Press the sides well to secure them in place.

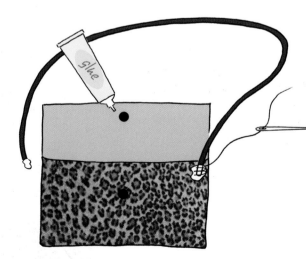

▶▶ **STEP 5** With the flap open, use gem glue to attach one end of the cord onto each side of the bag. Let dry. For extra strength, sew a few stitches through the cord with a needle and thread.

▶▶ **STEP 6** Use gem glue to add disk magnets or Velcro dots to the flap. (Make sure the magnets or dots are perfectly lined up so the flap will close correctly.) Let dry with the flap open.

▶▶ **STEP 7** If you want, use gem glue to add a decorative button to the front.

sock coin purse

Take an ordinary sock from drab to fab with just a few snips and stitches. There couldn't be a better way to make use of a lonely sock whose partner has mysteriously disappeared in the laundry!

what you need

- sock
- round shoelace
- liquid seam sealant (No-Fray Glue or Fray Check)
- fabric glue
- embroidery floss or thread
- fabric scissors
- decorative bead trim (optional)

▶▶ **STEP 1** With your fabric scissors, cut the top off of the sock a few inches above the heel.

▶▶ **STEP 2** Apply seam sealant around the cut edge of the sock to prevent fraying. Let dry.

▶▶ **STEP 3** Turn the sock inside out. Whipstitch the glued edges together to make the bottom of the purse (see The Whipped Stitch, page 17). Knot the thread and snip off any extra.

▶▶ **STEP 4** Turn the sock right-side-out. Thread a shoelace around the top of the sock, weaving the shoelace in and out of the fabric as shown. Stretch the sock as you poke the end of the shoelace through the weave of the sock. When you're done, tie the two ends of the shoelace together in a knot. Pull the lace from both sides to close the top of the bag.

▶▶ **STEP 5** If you want, use fabric glue to attach beaded trim around the bottom of the bag, or hang beads from the shoelace for decoration.

This colorful beach bag can carry seaside essentials like sunscreen and sunglasses. And the bag is so easy to make—all you do is weave two placemats together with lacing and then glue on a big fabric flower.

what you need

- 2 oval-shaped plastic woven placemats
- round plastic lacing, 3 yards
- scissors
- gem glue
- fabric flower
- wax paper

▶▶ **STEP 1**
Take one of the placemats and cut about 3 inches off of each end. Throw away the ends.

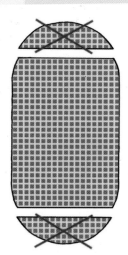

▶▶ **STEP 2**
Take the other placemat and cut a 1-inch-wide strip down the middle. This will be the purse handle. Throw away the rest of the placemat.

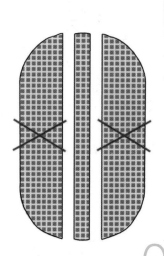

▶▶ STEP 3 Fold the first placemat in half to make the purse.

▶▶ STEP 4 Make a knot at one end of the lacing. Starting at one bottom corner, whipstitch up the side of the purse (see page 17). Stitch through every other hole, stitching the sides together. Continue until you are about 1 inch from the top.

▶▶ STEP 5 Fold the handle piece in half length-wise. With the creased side facing down, stick the handle inside the purse. Continue lacing, sewing the side and handle together.

what to stash in your bag for a day at the beach

✔ sunglasses
✔ sunscreen
✔ lip balm
✔ hairbrush
✔ cell phone
✔ book or diary

▶▶ STEP 6 Continue lacing around the handle, sewing it closed, until you are about 1 inch from the other end. Slip the end of the handle into the other side of the purse and lace down the side until you reach the bottom corner. Tie a knot in the lacing and snip off any extra.

▶▶ STEP 7 Put a piece of wax paper inside the purse. Glue the fabric flower onto the purse using gem glue.

▶▶ STEP 8 Lay the purse on its back and let dry overnight.

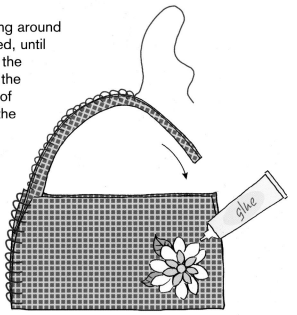

bag-along
felt purse

This soft felt purse is perfect to go anywhere, anytime. It looks just as good with blue jeans as with a mini and boots. Felt is super-simple to sew and is available in lots of eye-popping colors.

what you need

- 6 x 12-inch piece of felt
- embroidery floss or craft thread in contrasting color
- embroidery needle
- button
- cord, about 24 inches
- white craft glue
- ruler
- straight pins
- fabric scissors
- sheet of wax paper or plastic wrap

▶▶ **STEP 1** Lay the felt flat on the table in front of you. Fold one short end up 4 inches from the edge, as shown. The remaining, top portion of the felt is for the flap of the purse. Trim the corners of the flap to make them round.

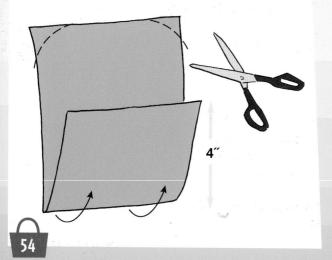

4″

▶▶ **STEP 2** Pin the folded section in place, as shown. Starting at one bottom corner, sew up the side of the purse, stitching the layers together, using a blanket stitch (see "how to do the blanket stitch," opposite). Continue sewing around the flap and down the other side until you reach the opposite corner. Tie the floss in a knot and snip off the extra.

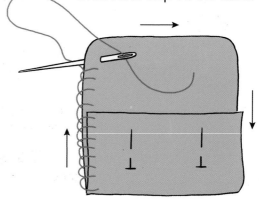

STEP 3 Cut a slit in the center of the top flap, wide enough for the button to fit through. Sew around the slit with a blanket stitch for decoration.

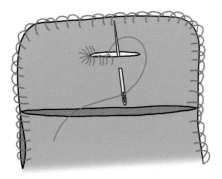

how to do the blanket stitch

The blanket stitch is used to sew two edges together or to attach an appliqué. It is called the "buttonhole stitch" when the stitches are sewn close together.

STEP 1 Thread the needle and knot the long end (see page 17). Poke the needle through the front of the fabric, close to the edge. Pull the needle until the thread goes all the way through.

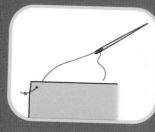

STEP 2 Move your hand over a bit and poke the needle back through the front of the fabric. Bring the sharp end of the needle through the looped thread in the back, as shown. Pull gently until the thread stops.

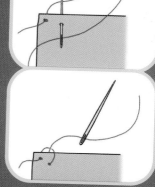

STEP 3 Repeat step 2, working your way along the edge of the fabric. Be sure your stitches are evenly spaced. Keep going until you reach the end. Knot the thread close to the fabric and snip off any extra.

STEP 4 Fold the flap over and make a small pen mark through the center of the buttonhole. This will tell you where to sew the button. Open the flap and sew the button on top of the pen mark.

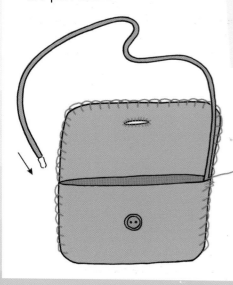

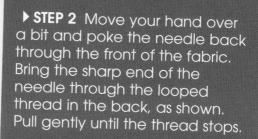

STEP 5 Cut the cord to the length you want for the strap (drape the cord over your shoulder to find the best length). Dip each end of the cord in white glue. Let the cord dry on a sheet of wax paper or plastic wrap.

STEP 6 Sew the ends of the cord to the top inside corners of the purse.

color blocks

geometric felt purse

Yeah, baby! These mod-looking bags will add sizzle and spice to your latest look. Mix and match an assortment of bright colored felt fabrics to make your own one-of-a-kind purse.

what you need

- 9 x 7-inch piece of felt
- assorted pieces of felt in different colors, cut into squares or other shapes
- fabric glue
- embroidery floss or craft thread in contrasting color
- embroidery needle
- button
- cord, about 24 inches
- white craft glue
- ruler
- straight pins
- fabric scissors
- sheet of wax paper or plastic wrap

▶▶ **STEP 1** Lay the felt flat on the table in front of you, with one of the short sides nearest you. Decorate the top half with square pieces of felt in contrasting colors. Use a small dot of fabric glue to attach each shape. (You can also use other fun shapes, like triangles, circles, and hearts.) Let the glue dry completely.

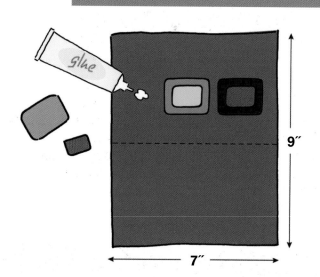

▶▶ STEP 2 With embroidery needle and floss or thread, sew around the shapes with a blanket stitch for decoration (see page 55).

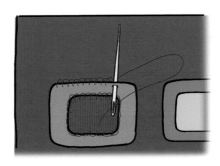

▶▶ STEP 3 Fold the felt in half to make the purse. Starting at one bottom corner, use the blanket stitch to sew up one side, stitching the sides together. Continue stitching across the top through one layer of felt. You don't want to stitch the purse shut! Make a knot and clip the thread at the top corner. Stitch the other edge and top, repeating what you did for the other side.

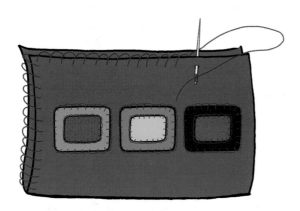

▶▶ STEP 4 Cut the cord to the length you want for the strap (drape the cord over your shoulder to find the best length). Dip each end of the cord in white glue. Let the cord dry on a sheet of wax paper or plastic wrap. Sew the ends of the cord to the top inside corners of the purse (see illustration on page 55).

what to stash in your bag
for a day at school
✔ pencil and pen
✔ small pad
✔ pocket calculator
✔ comb or brush
✔ compact mirror
✔ lip gloss
✔ lunch/snack money

cell mate

embroidered cell phone bag

This cell phone bag will do the talking for you! It's made from oh-so-soft felt and spiffed up with pretty embroidery stiches. There's even a handy key chain attached to bag.

what you need

- two 3 x 5-inch pieces of felt in the same color
- embroidery floss or craft thread in contrasting colors
- embroidery needle
- 24-inch long piece of cord
- white craft glue
- ruler
- straight pins
- scissors
- pencil
- sheet of wax paper or plastic wrap

▶▶ **STEP 1** Use a pencil to draw swirly designs on each piece of felt. You can copy the design in the photo or make up your own.

▶▶ **STEP 2** Sew along the lines with your embroidery needle and embroidery floss or thread using a running stitch (see page 17) or chain stitch (see "how to do the chain stitch," page 60).

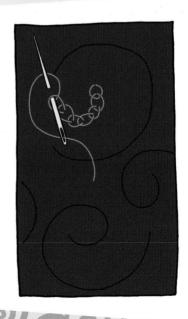

▶▶ STEP 3 Lay the two pieces of felt back to back, with the designs on the outside and the tops lined up. Starting at the right top corner, sew down the side using the blanket stitch (see page 55) and going through both layers of felt. Continue blanket stitching around the bottom and up the other side, going through both layers of felt. Continue stitching across the top, going through only one layer of felt (you don't want to sew the purse shut). When you reach the top corner, keep stitching around the other top edge of the felt, so both top edges are decorated. When you finish, knot the floss or thread and snip off any extra.

▶▶ STEP 4 Cut the cord to the length you want for the strap (drape the cord over your shoulder to find the best length). Dip each end of the cord in white glue. Let dry on a sheet of wax paper or plastic wrap.

▶▶ STEP 5 Sew the ends of the cord to the top inside corners of the purse (see illustration on page 55).

▶▶ STEP 6 Make a key chain by cutting a smaller piece of cord, about 3 or 4 inches long. Dip the ends in white glue and let dry. Fold the piece of cord in half to form a loop, then sew the ends inside the purse with the loop hanging out.

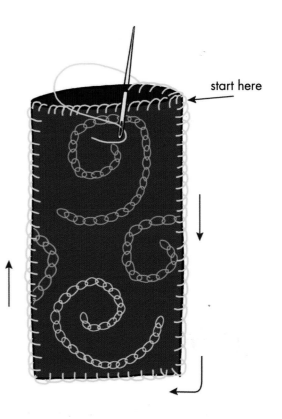

start here

how to do the chain stitch

A chain stitch is a decorative embroidery stitch. Use an embroidery needle and embroidery floss or craft thread in a contrasting color (a color very different from the color of the fabric) so the stitchwork stands out.

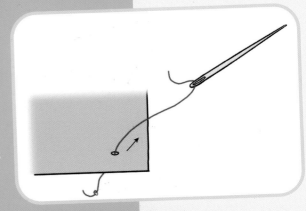

▶ Step 1 Thread the needle and knot the long end. Poke the needle through the fabric and pull the thread until it goes all the way through to the knot.

▶ Step 2 Make a loop with the thread. Poke the needle close to where the thread comes out of the fabric, then back out a short distance away, as shown. Keep the loop of thread under the tip of the needle. Pull the thread to form the first chain stitch.

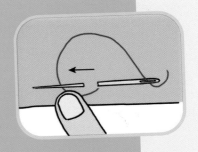

▶ Step 3 Make a loop for the next stitch. Poke the needle **inside** of the loop of the last stitch you made, right next to where the thread is coming out of the fabric.

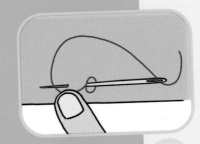

▶ Step 4 Continue making chain stitches along the lines of your design until you reach the end. Poke the needle on the outside of the last loop in the chain, close to the top of the loop. Make a knot on the wrong side of the fabric. Clip the thread.

outside the box

stationery box bag

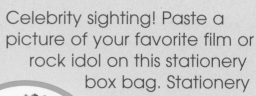

ART chix Studio

Celebrity sighting! Paste a picture of your favorite film or rock idol on this stationery box bag. Stationery boxes are colorful and sturdy, and the perfect size for purses. Look for boxes, beads, and trims in your local arts and crafts store.

what you need

- stationery box (a sturdy cardboard box with attached hinged lid)
- magazine cut-out of movie star or celebrity
- colored paper
- glue stick
- découpage glue
- paintbrush for glue
- beaded trim, gems, and sequins
- 2 paper fasteners

- gem glue
- large needle or needle tool
- string, 12 inches
- plastic coated wire, 18 inches
- large plastic beads
- 2 small beads or buttons
- scissors
- old scissors or nail clippers

▶▶ **STEP 1** Cut colored paper to fit the front of your box. With a glue stick, glue your picture onto the paper, then glue the paper onto the front of the box.

▶▶ **STEP 2** Use a paintbrush to coat the picture and paper with a thin layer of découpage glue. This will seal and protect the surface of the box. Let dry overnight.

STEP 3 Poke two holes in the top of the box for the handle.

STEP 4 Slip a bead or button onto one end of the wire. Twist the wire around itself to keep the button in place. Poke the other end of the wire up through one of the holes in the box for the purse handle. The bead or button will keep the wire from pulling out.

STEP 5 Slide beads onto the wire to make a handle. Poke the other end of the wire through the second hole and secure with another bead or button inside the box. Clip off any extra wire with old scissors or nail clippers.

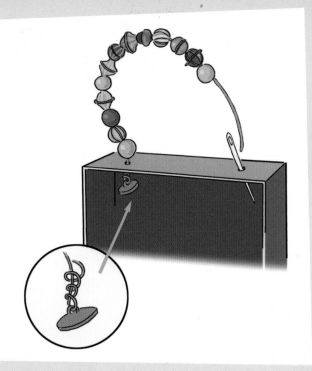

STEP 6 Poke one hole in the top and one hole in the lid, as shown, for the closure. Put a paper fastener in each hole and bend open the legs to secure.

STEP 7 Tie string around one of the fasteners and knot tightly. Leave 8 inches of string for closing the purse. Close the purse by twisting the string around the fasteners in a figure-eight pattern.

STEP 8 Decorate the front of the bag with gems, beaded trim, and sequins using gem glue. Let dry overnight.

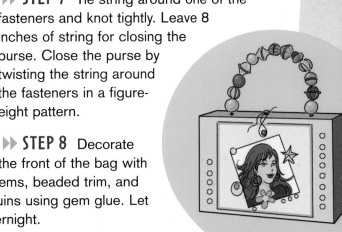

bring it on

nothing can stop you now

You go, girl! You've learned all the tricks and now you want a real challenge. The projects in this chapter may take a little more time and patience, but the rewards will make it all worthwhile. You'll see how to make the most of unusual materials, like duct tape and newspaper—even plastic grocery bags! So, get ready to score some style points with the hottest handbags around.

vintage visions

collage tote

These totes have a retro look that is so right now. Collage papers in antique prints can be bought in craft stores. You can also make the bags from wrapping paper, newspaper, or any paper you like!

Collage Papers™ by DMD, Inc. Paper Reflections®

▶▶ **STEP 1** Lay the decorative paper face-up on the table.

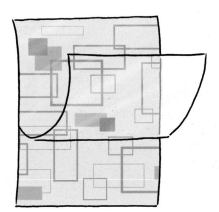

▶▶ **STEP 2** Peel the top edge of the protective paper off the heavyweight sheet of laminate. Carefully press the laminate onto the paper, matching up the top edges and corners. Press the laminate onto the collage paper, smoothing out the air bubbles and peeling off the protective paper as you go.

▶▶ **STEP 3** Press the lightweight laminate sheet onto the other side of the paper, matching the top edges and corners. Use both hands to line the sheets up evenly. Press out any air bubbles, peeling and pressing as you did in step 2.

▶▶ STEP 4 Photocopy the pattern on page 69 to the percentage shown and cut out, or use the pattern as a measuring guide. Keep the paper face-down and transfer all of the pattern markings.

▶▶ STEP 5 Cut out triangle shapes as shown. (This will make the sides easier to fold.)

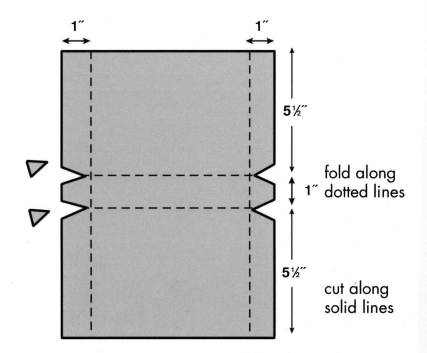

1″   1″

5½″

fold along
1″ dotted lines

5½″

cut along
solid lines

▶▶ STEP 6 Fold the laminated paper along the dotted lines to make the purse. Fold all of the sections in the same direction (toward the inside of the purse). Press the folds to make sharp creases.

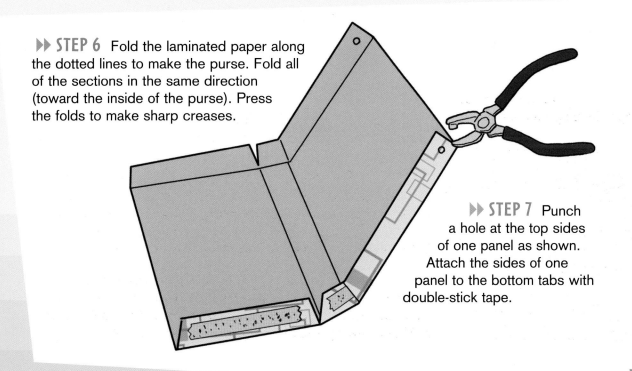

▶▶ STEP 7 Punch a hole at the top sides of one panel as shown. Attach the sides of one panel to the bottom tabs with double-stick tape.

▶▶ STEP 8 Bring up the other panel and tape the sides together with a strip of tape to hold in place. One side will completely cover the other. Line up your hole punch through the holes you already made and punch through the second layer of paper.

▶▶ STEP 9 Thread the ends of the beaded trim or cord through the holes on the sides of the bag. Knot the ends inside the bag to keep the handle in place. Dab white glue on the knots to secure them.

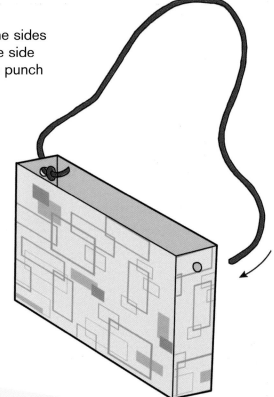

try this!
Instead of having one purse handle that comes from the sides of the bag, you can punch holes in the front and back for a pair of handles. Use a ruler to make sure the handles are matched up perfectly.

NOTE: copy at 150%

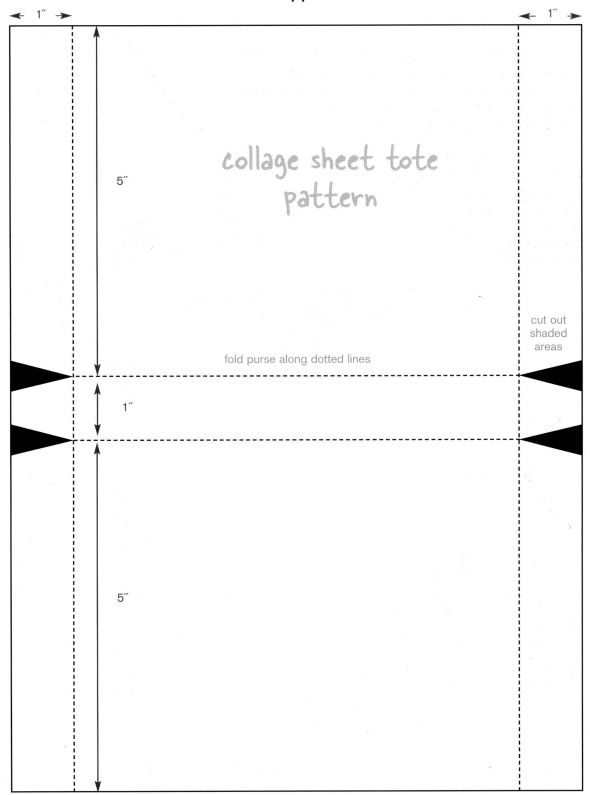

1″

1″

5″

collage sheet tote
pattern

cut out
shaded
areas

fold purse along dotted lines

1″

5″

seeing things

clear flower purse

Your friends won't believe their eyes when you show them this clearly beautiful purse. Made from dried, pressed flowers, it has a fresh-from-the-garden look that's perfect for spring or summer. All of the supplies are easy to find in arts and crafts stores.

what you need

- 2 small packages of dried, pressed flowers
- two 9 x 12-inch sheets of clear heavyweight laminating film
- 4 colored paper fasteners
- string or floss, about 12 inches
- cord, 36 inches long
- double-sided tape
- pen
- ruler
- scissors
- round hole-punch
- large tapestry or embroidery needle

▶▶ **STEP 1** Work on a flat surface. Peel the protective paper off of one sheet of laminate. Place the clear sheet on the table with the sticky side up.

▶▶ **STEP 2** Decorate the sticky laminate with pressed flowers.

▶▶ **STEP 3** Peel off one edge of the protective paper from the other sheet of laminate. Carefully press the sticky sides together over the flowers, matching the corners and edges. Continue to peel the rest of the protective paper away, pressing as you go. Smooth out any air bubbles, pressing over the whole sheet with your hand.

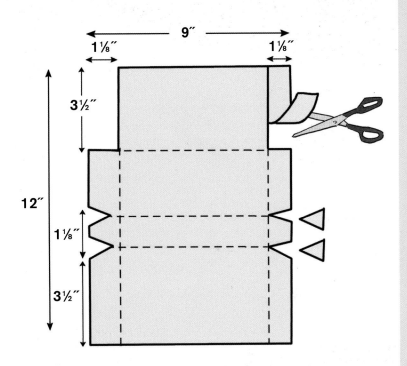

STEP 4 Photocopy the pattern on page 73 to the percentage shown and cut out, or use the pattern as a measuring guide. Transfer all pattern markings and cut out the shaded areas, as shown.

cut rounded corners

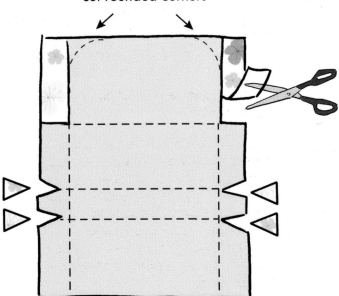

STEP 5 Lay the pattern over the clear laminate and cut around the pattern. To round the edges of the purse flap, trace around the edge of a small drinking cup and cut out.

STEP 6 Fold the laminate along the fold lines to make the purse. Fold all of the sections in the same direction (toward the inside of the purse). Press the folds to crease.

STEP 7 Punch a hole at the top sides of one panel as shown. Attach the sides of one panel to the bottom tabs with double-stick tape.

STEP 8 Bring up the other panel and tape the sides together with a strip of tape to hold in place. One side will completely cover the other. Line up your hole punch through the holes you already made and punch through the second layer.

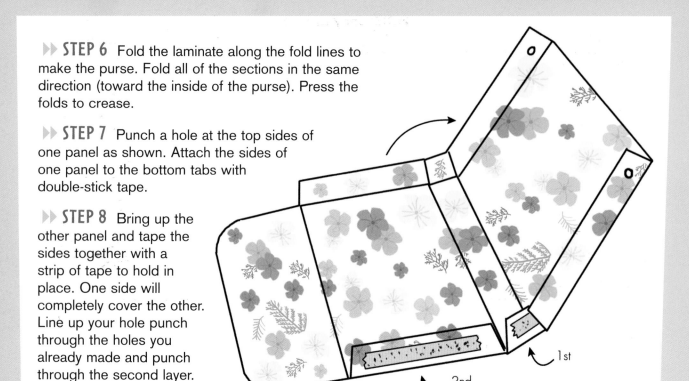

1st

2nd

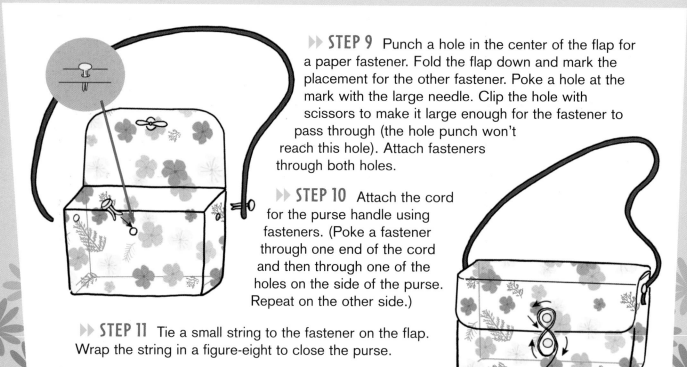

STEP 9 Punch a hole in the center of the flap for a paper fastener. Fold the flap down and mark the placement for the other fastener. Poke a hole at the mark with the large needle. Clip the hole with scissors to make it large enough for the fastener to pass through (the hole punch won't reach this hole). Attach fasteners through both holes.

STEP 10 Attach the cord for the purse handle using fasteners. (Poke a fastener through one end of the cord and then through one of the holes on the side of the purse. Repeat on the other side.)

STEP 11 Tie a small string to the fastener on the flap. Wrap the string in a figure-eight to close the purse.

NOTE: copy at 150%

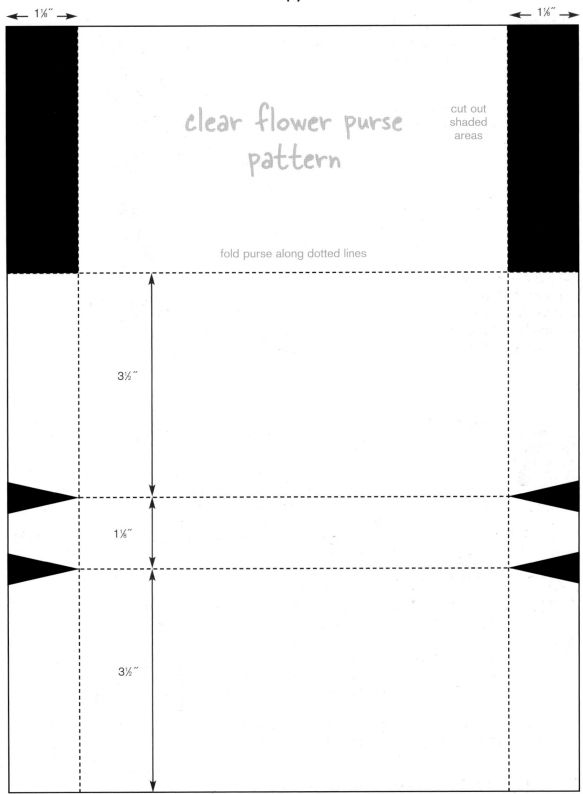

← 1⅛″ →   ← 1⅛″ →

clear flower purse
pattern

cut out
shaded
areas

fold purse along dotted lines

3½″

1⅛″

3½″

news flash
laminated newspaper bag

You'll make fashion headlines with this laminated newspaper bag. Look for newspaper pages with lots of interesting headlines and pictures, or choose a paper dated to a special day, like a birthday or graduation. You'll not only have a super cool bag, you'll have a happy reminder of the big event.

what you need

- two 9 x 12-inch sheets of clear laminating film (1 lightweight and 1 heavyweight)
- sheet newspaper
- 2 paper fasteners
- chain from a hardware store or cord
- double-stick tape
- pen
- ruler
- scissors
- round hole-punch
- large embroidery or tapestry needle

▶▶ **STEP 1** Lay the newspaper face-up on a flat table.

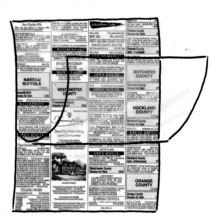

▶▶ **STEP 2**
Peel the top edge of the protective paper off the heavyweight sheet of laminate. Carefully press the laminate onto the newspaper, smoothing out the air bubbles and peeling the protective paper off as you go.

▶▶ **STEP 3** Press the lightweight laminate sheet onto the other side of the newspaper, matching the top edge and corners. Use both hands to line the sheets up evenly. Press out any air bubbles, peeling and pressing as you did in step 2.

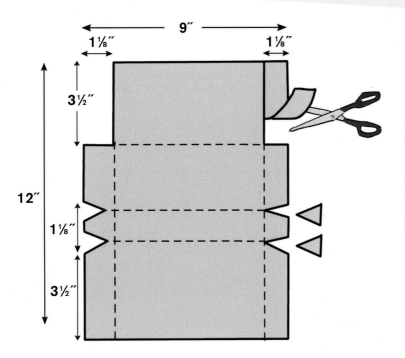

▶▶ STEP 4 Photocopy the pattern on page 77 to the percentage shown and cut it out, or use the pattern as a measuring guide. Transfer all pattern markings and cut out the shaded areas, as shown.

▶▶ STEP 5 Lay the pattern over the clear laminate and cut around the pattern. (Hint: If you are making your own pattern, trace the pointed flap of an envelope and cut out to make pointed purse flap.)

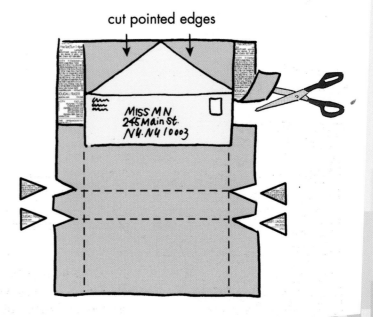

cut pointed edges

STEP 6 Fold the laminate along the fold lines. Punch a hole at the top sides of one panel as shown. Attach the sides of one panel to the bottom tabs with double-stick tape. Bring up the other panel and tape the sides together with a strip of tape to hold in place. One side will completely cover the other. Line up your hole punch through the holes you already made and punch through the second layer of laminated paper.

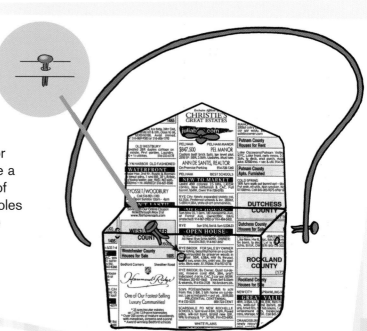

1st

2nd

STEP 7 Punch a hole in the center of the flap for a paper fastener. Fold the flap down and mark the placement for the other fastener. Poke a hole at the mark with the large needle. Clip the hole with scissors to make it large enough for the fastener to pass through (the hole punch won't reach this hole). Attach fasteners through both holes.

STEP 8 Attach the cord or chain for the purse handle using fasteners. (Poke a fastener through the chain or one end of the cord and then through one of the holes on the side of the purse. Repeat on the other side.)

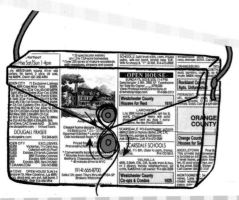

STEP 9 Tie a small string to one of the fasteners on the flap. Wrap the string in a figure-eight to close the purse.

NOTE: copy at 150%

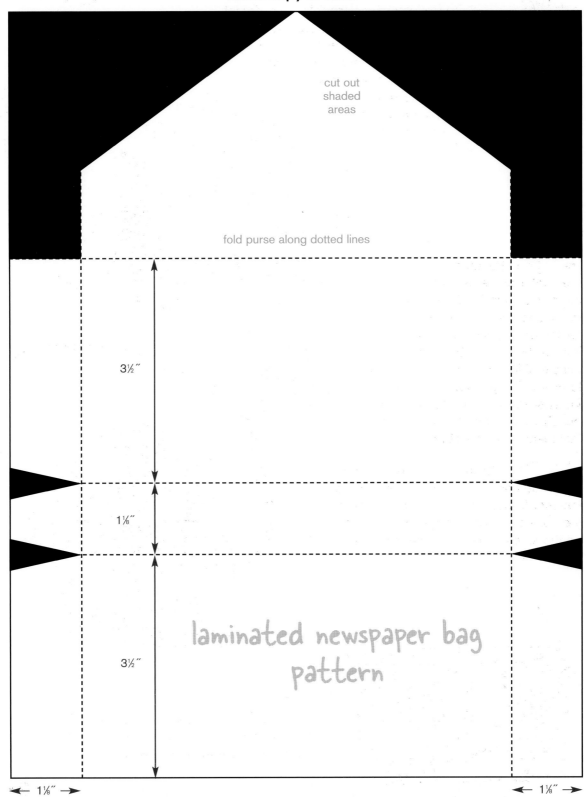

cut out
shaded
areas

fold purse along dotted lines

3½″

1⅛″

laminated newspaper bag
pattern

3½″

← 1⅛″ →

← 1⅛″ →

stick to it

duct tape bag

Sleek and chic, who would guess this bag is made from everyday duct tape. Duct tape can be easily found in grocery, hardware, and variety stores. Pair the silver purse with casual clothes for an instant flash of high fashion.

what you need

- roll of silver duct tape, 2 inches wide
- roll of silver duct tape, .70 inches wide ("skinny" tape)
- 3 sheets of 8 1/2 by 11 inch paper (printer paper or copy paper)
- scissors
- magnets (optional)

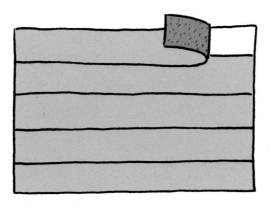

hot tip

Work on a smooth surface, such as a plastic cutting board or non-stick countertop.

▶▶ **STEP 1** Cover both sides of each sheet of paper with the thick duct tape. Overlap each piece of tape slightly over the last until the entire sheet is covered with tape.

▶▶ **STEP 2** Use the pattern on page 81 or draw your own 7 x 9-inch rectangle on two of the sheets of tape-covered paper. Cut out the rectangles.

▶▶ **STEP 3** Photocopy the patterns on page 80 to the percentage shown or use the pattern as a measuring guide to cut three strips from the third sheet of tape-covered paper. (The strips are for the bottom and sides of the purse.)

STEP 4 Make a sheet of duct tape for the flap. Overlap 2-inch-wide strips of tape to make the sheet as you did in steps 1 and 2, except do not use paper in between the layers of tape. This will make a flexible flap. Start by overlapping strips of tape, sticky sides up, to make a sheet. Then, cover the sticky side of the sheet with more strips. Cut this sheet 9 x 7 inches. Cut the corners to make them round.

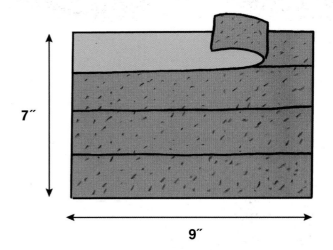

7″

9″

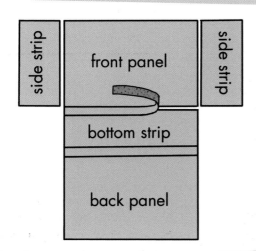

side strip

front panel

side strip

bottom strip

back panel

STEP 5 Arrange the strips and panels as shown. Use pieces of skinny tape to tape all of the sections together. Flip the entire piece over and apply skinny tape over the seams on the back side. Trim off any loose tape ends.

STEP 6 Fold the panels into place to form the purse, taping them together on the **inside** as you go. Work slowly, taping as neatly as possible. (You can lift and move the tape as needed.)

STEP 7 Now, cover the seams on the outside with skinny tape. Trim the ends of the tape.

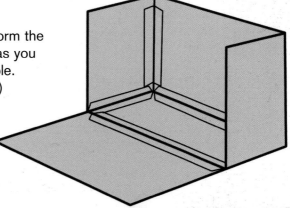

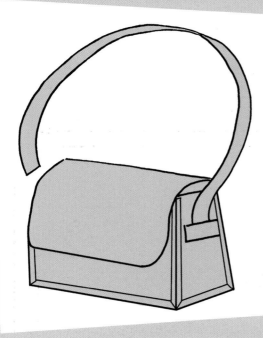

▶▶ **STEP 8** Use tape to attach the flap piece to the back panel.

▶▶ **STEP 9** To make the strap, roll out a long piece of the thick duct tape. Fold the strip in half lengthwise. (Hint: Let the roll hang as you fold the strip in half. This will help keep the tape from sticking to itself and getting wrinkled.) Cut the tape when you are happy with the length of the strap. Tape the strap to the sides of the purse. If you want, tape a magnet to the inside of the flap and another to the front of the purse to secure the flap in place.

NOTE: copy at 150%

strip for bottom
2″ x 9″

strip for side
2″ x 7″

strip for side
2″ x 7″

duct tape
bag
pattern
(bottom
& sides)

NOTE: copy at 150%

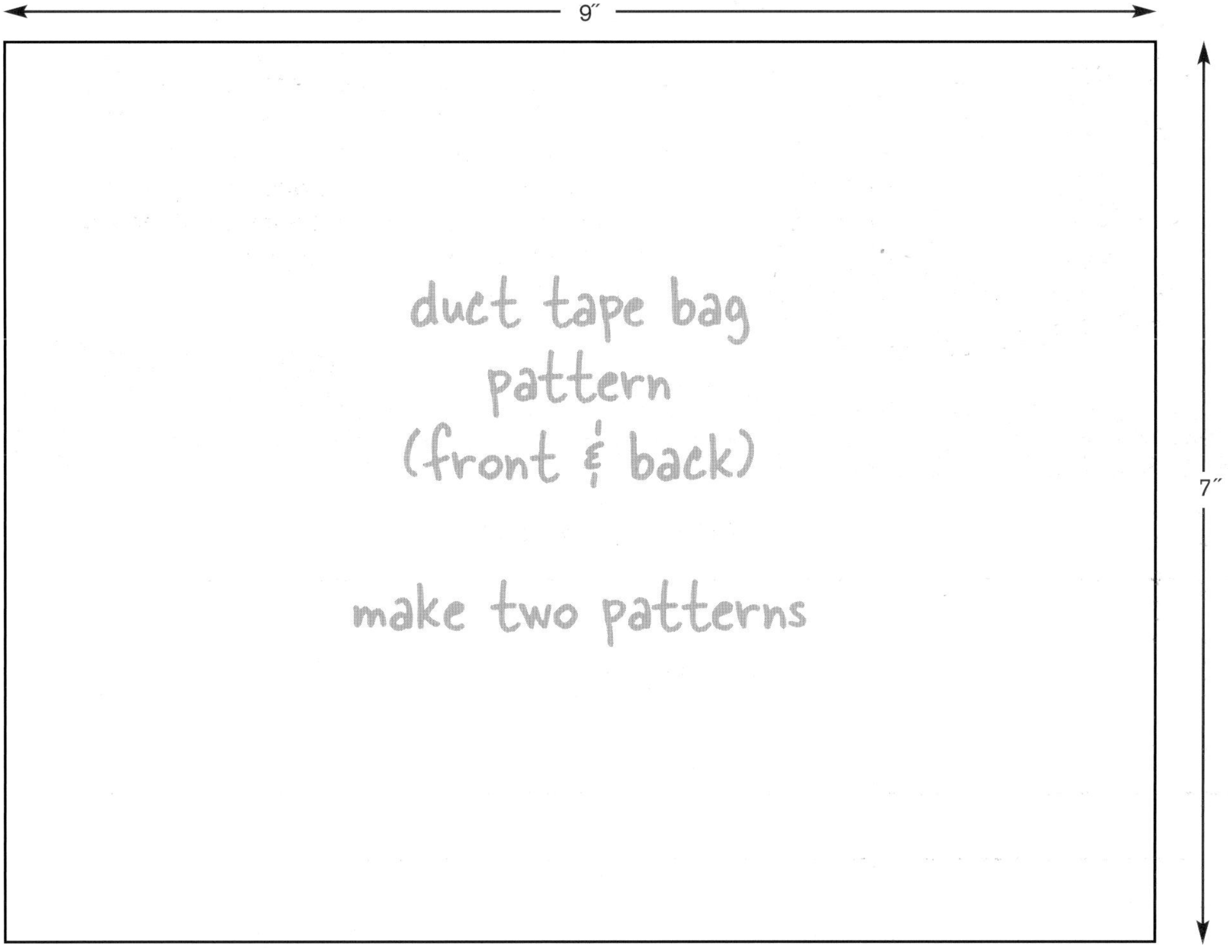

9″
7″
duct tape bag
pattern
(front & back)
make two patterns

hot tip

If you want, you can decorate the purse with stickers or permanent markers.

quick silver

trapezoid duct tape bag

Metallic accessories add sparkle and shimmer to everything from blue jeans to dresses. Be the trendsetter among your crowd with this stylish silver purse. We've made it extra big and roomy so you can carry everything you need.

what you need

- roll of silver duct tape, 2 inches wide
- roll of silver duct tape, .70 inches wide ("skinny" tape)
- 3 sheets of 8½ x 11-inch paper (printer paper or copy paper)
- scissors

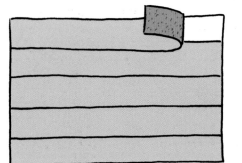

▶▶ **STEP 1** Cover both sides of each sheet of paper with the thick duct tape. Overlap each piece of tape slightly over the last until the entire sheet is covered with tape.

▶▶ **STEP 2** Photocopy the pattern on page 85 to the percentage shown or use the pattern as a measuring guide to draw a trapezoid shape on two of the tape-covered sheets. Cut out the two trapezoid shapes for the front and back of the purse.

▶▶ **STEP 3** Photocopy the patterns on page 84 to the percentage shown or use the pattern as a measuring guide to cut three strips from the third sheet of tape-covered paper. (The strips are for the bottom and sides of the purse.)

▶▶ STEP 4 Cut two 2 x 9-inch strips of the thick duct tape. Carefully line them up, sticky sides facing each other, to make one double-sided strip of tape. Cut the corners off of one end of the strip, as shown. This is the tab you will use to close the purse.

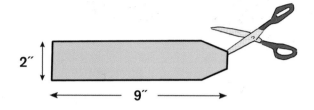

2″

9″

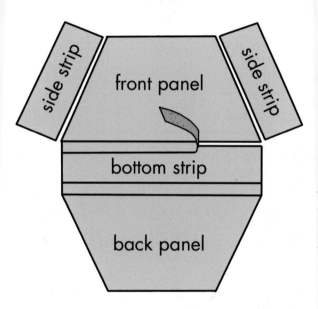

side strip

front panel

side strip

bottom strip

back panel

▶▶ STEP 5 Arrange the bottom and side strips to the panels as shown. Use pieces of skinny tape to tape the sections together. Flip the entire thing over and put skinny tape over the seams on the back. Trim off any loose tape ends.

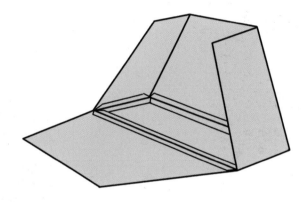

▶▶ STEP 6 Fold the panels into place to form the purse, taping them together on the **inside** as you go. Work slowly, taping as neatly as possible. (You can lift and move the tape as needed.)

▶▶ STEP 7 Now, cover the seams on the outside with skinny tape. Trim the ends of the tape.

▶▶ STEP 8 Use a strip of tape to attach the closure tab to the back of the purse (this is the 2 x 9-inch double-sided strip).

▶▶ **STEP 9** Cut a 4-inch-long strip of skinny tape. Cut another strip, this time 3 inches long. Lay the shorter strip in the center of the longer one, sticky sides together. You should end up with a double-sided strip with a sticky part on each end. Attach this strip to the front of your purse, as shown. Slide the closure strip through this front strip to close the purse.

▶▶ **STEP 10** To make the strap, roll out a long piece of the thick duct tape. Fold the strip in half lengthwise. (Hint: Let the roll hang as you fold the strip in half. This will help keep the tape from sticking to itself and getting wrinkled.) Cut the tape when you are happy with the length of the strap. Tape the strap to the sides of the purse.

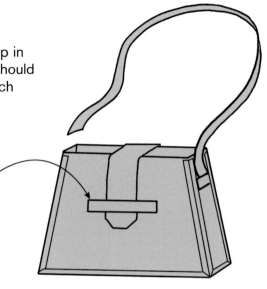

NOTE: copy at 150%

strip for bottom
2″ x 10″

strip for side
2″ x 7″

strip for side
2″ x 7″

trapezoid
duct tape
bag
pattern
(bottom
& sides)

NOTE: copy at 150%

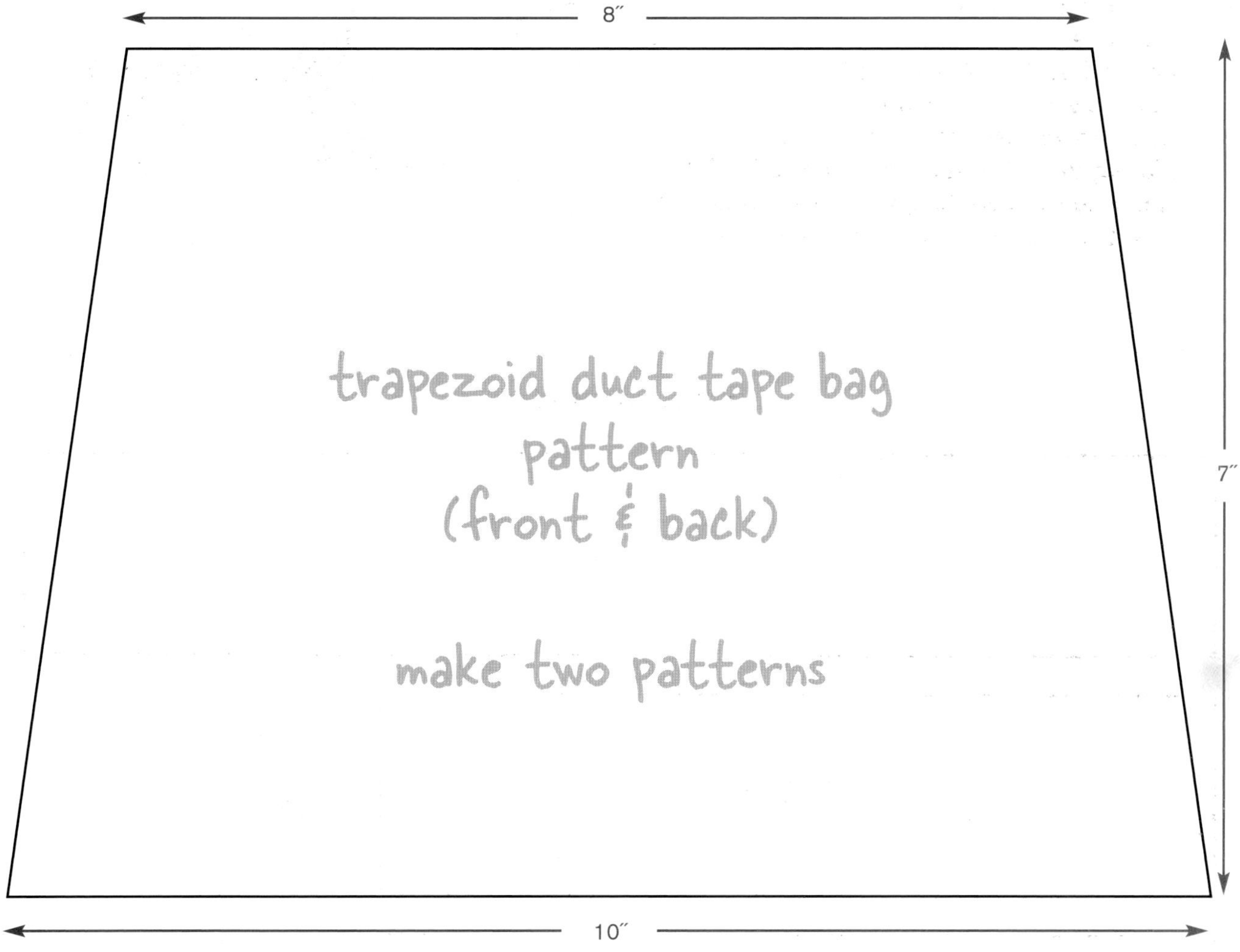

8″

7″

trapezoid duct tape bag
pattern
(front & back)

make two patterns

10″

Project by Rachel Pfeffer

Thick or thin, stripes are the perfect pick-me-up. Follow fashion's fine line with this striped duct tape purse. It's a snap to make using rolls of brown and red duct tape, sold in many hardware and department stores.

what you need

- roll of brown duct tape, 2 inches wide
- roll of red duct tape, .70 inches wide ("skinny" tape)
- 3 sheets of 8½ x 11-inch paper (printer paper or copy paper)
- paper
- scissors

▶▶ **STEP 1** Cover both sides of each sheet of paper with the brown duct tape. Overlap each piece of tape slightly over the last until the entire sheet is covered with tape.

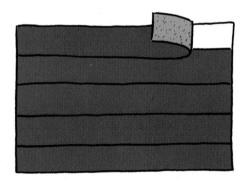

▶▶ **STEP 3** Photocopy the pattern on page 89 to the percentage shown or use the pattern as a measuring guide to draw a trapezoid shape on two of the tape-covered sheets. Cut out the two trapezoid shapes for the front and back of the purse.

▶▶ **STEP 3** Photocopy the patterns on page 88 to the percentage shown or use the pattern as a measuring guide to cut three strips from the third sheet of tape-covered paper. (The strips are for the bottom and sides of the purse.)

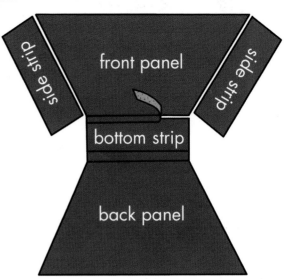

▶▶ **STEP 4** Arrange the bottom and side strips to the panels as shown. Use pieces of skinny tape to tape all of the sections together. Flip the entire thing over and tape over the seams on the back side. Trim off any loose tape ends.

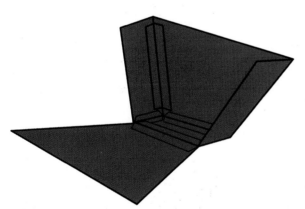

▶▶ **STEP 5** Fold the panels into place to form the purse, taping them together on the **inside** as you go. Work slowly, taping as neatly as possible. (You can lift and move the tape as needed.)

▶▶ **STEP 6** Now, cover the seams on the outside with brown tape. Trim the ends of the tape.

▶▶ **STEP 7** Decorate the front of the purse with stripes of red duct tape.

▶▶ **STEP 8** Decide how long you want your strap to be. Cut two strips of brown tape. Press the two strips together, sticky sides facing. (If you want, you can make one side red instead of brown.) For decoration, lay a strip of red skinny tape along the center of the brown side of the strap. Tape the strap to the sides of the purse.

A

B

▶▶ **STEP 10** To make a bow, cut a ¾-inch-long strip of red tape. Fold the strip in half lengthwise, sticky sides together. Make two loops, criss-cross the ends, and pinch the center (A). Tape the center of the loops with a piece of tape (B) and tape the bow to the front of the purse.

NOTE: copy at 150%

trapezoid duct tape bag pattern (bottom & sides)

strip for bottom
2″ x 5″

strip for side
2″ x 8″

strip for side
2″ x 8″

NOTE: copy at 150%

9″

striped duct tape bag
pattern
(front & back)

make two patterns

8″

5″

plastic fantastic

grocery bag purse

Take everyday plastic shopping bags from trash to treasure with this easy weaving technique. Plastic bags are fun to work with and they're very strong and sturdy—they're even waterproof so you can carry the bag on rainy days without worry.

what you need

- 3 clean small white plastic shopping bags
- 4 clean small red plastic shopping bags (you can also use blue, black, or any other color)
- 8 x 7-inch piece of cardboard
- scissors
- ruler
- pencil
- shoelace

hot tip

Don't worry if there is printing on your bags. This makes cool specks of color on the finished purse.

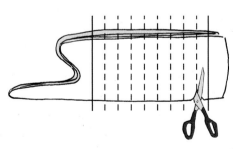

▶▶ **STEP 1** Smooth and flatten the bags. Stack the three white bags and fold them in half lengthwise. Cut the bags into strips, going across the width of the bags. Each strip should be about an inch wide. Throw away the tops and bottoms. You should end up with lots of ring-shaped strips.

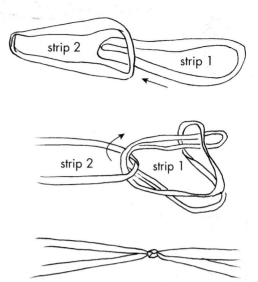

▶▶ **STEP 2** Pick up two strips. Loop strip #1 through strip #2, as shown. Then run strip #1 back through its own end. Pull the strips gently until they are tight, but not too tight or they will tear.

▶▶ **STEP 3** Pick up another plastic strip. Repeat step 2, looping this new strip onto the end of strip 1 and making a knot. (Basically, you're making a "chain" of the plastic strips.) Keep looping on strips, one after the other, until you have several linked together. This is your white "yarn." Add more strips as you need them.

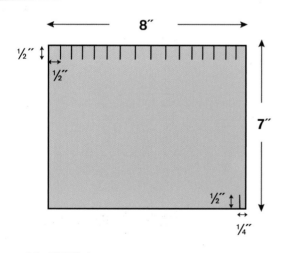

▶▶ **STEP 4** Mark and cut slits across the top of the cardboard, ½ inch wide and ½ inch long. You will have fifteen slits when you're finished. Cut one slit in the lower right corner, ¼ inch from the right side and about ½ inch long. This is your "loom."

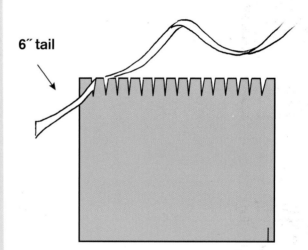

▶▶ **STEP 5** To start weaving, slip the end of the white yarn in the first slit on the upper left of your loom. Leave about a 6-inch-long tail hanging out the front.

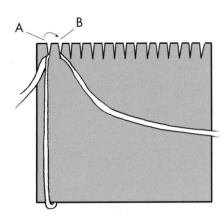

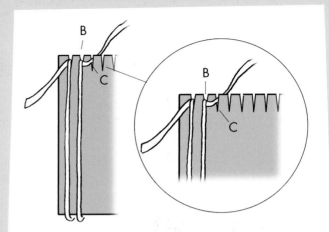

▶▶ **STEP 6** Wrap the yarn around the cardboard loom and through the same slit at the top (A). Pull the yarn across the back of the cardboard and through to the next slit, bringing it to the front (B).

▶▶ **STEP 7** Wrap the yarn around the loom again and back through the second slit on top (B). Pull the yarn over and through to the next slit, this time pulling it across the **front** of the cardboard and through the slit to the back of the loom (C).

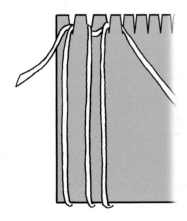

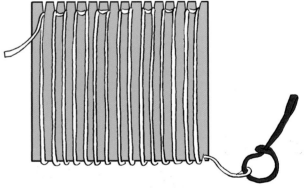

▶▶ **STEP 8** Continue wrapping the yarn as you did in steps 6 and 7, alternating from front to back as you go.

▶▶ **STEP 9** Finish by pulling the end of the yarn through the slit at the bottom of the cardboard, as shown. You should have fifteen strips of yarn on the front of the loom and sixteen on the back. These are called the "warp" strips.

▶▶ **STEP 10** Now, you will weave in colored "yarn" going across the white (these are the "weft" strips). Take your red plastic bags and follow step 1 to cut lots of ring-shaped strips. Start by adding a colored strip to the end of the last white strip, as you did in step 3. Add three or four more colored strips to give yourself enough yarn to weave.

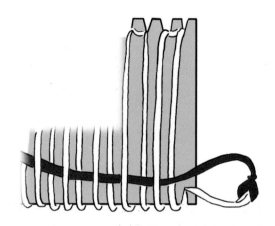

▶▶ **STEP 11** Start weaving over and under the white strips with the colored yarn. It helps to weave across the entire side before pulling the yarn through.

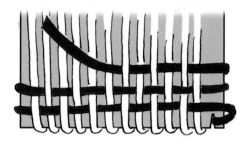

▶▶ **STEP 12** Flip the loom over and keep weaving around the back side. (Keep the same over under pattern going as you turn the loom over. For example: if you ended by going under on the first side, go over the yarn as you continue weaving around the back side.)

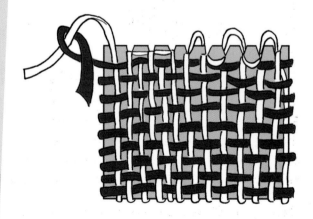

▶▶ **STEP 13** Weave back to the white tail you left at the beginning of step 6. Tie your colored yarn to the white tail to secure it in place.

▶▶ **STEP 14** Lift the loops off of the slits at the top of the loom. Slide the cardboard loom out of the woven purse. Weave the loose ends into the inside of the purse to hide them. Clip off the excess.

▶▶ **STEP 15** Tie the ends of the shoelace to the sides of the purse for a handle.

shop talk
where to go for what

ARTchix Stuido
250-370-9985
www.artchixstudio.com
vintage collage sheets,
charms, fasteners, findings

Con-Tact® brand
877-353-6410
www.contactbrand.com
self-adhesive laminate
coverings

DMD, Inc.
www.dmdind.com
collage Papers™, cardstock,
ribbon

Duck Tape®
www.ducktapeclub.com
duct tape and "skinny"
duct tape, 20 colors

Grafix®
216-581-9050
www.graphixarts.com
Laminating Film®
and Funky Fur®

Expo International, Inc.
Trimtations
(Available at large fabric,
craft, and variety stores.)
beaded trims, lace, leather
and pearls

**Jacquard Products/Rupert
Gibbon & Spider Inc.**
www.jacquardproducts.com
Lumiere® and Neopaque®
paints

Nature's Pressed
801-225-1169/
800-850-2499
www.naturespressed.com
pressed flowers and leaves

Toner Plastics
www.tonerplastics.com
Fun Wire™
and CraftLace™

Dare Food
Kitchener, Ontario
Canada N2G 4G4
1-800-668-3273
(Source of cookie bags
pictured on page 42.)